The Impact of Learning Management Systems on Student Satisfaction

By
Denise N. Fyffe

Jamaica Pen

A Needs Assessment Study on Staff Proficiency, System Usage, and Student Satisfaction

The Impact of Learning Management Systems on Student Satisfaction

Cover design by Denise N. Fyffe

Third Edition

Jamaica Pen Publishers

Table of Contents

Companies needlessly spend millions of dollars on initiatives to resolve productivity issues within their organisation. Often the solutions implemented compound the problem and doesn't resolve their core issues. To prevent such occurrences, it is necessary to conduct a Needs Assessment or Needs Analysis. This method allows a professional to analyse and identify the actual needs or gaps which may exist in an organisation. The process will present findings which will establish the gaps and recommendations can be made on how to fix these gaps. An organised or efficient approach will always garner greater benefits than an ill prepared method.

In this book we will utilise this method to conduct an "Appraisal of staff proficiency with the Learning Management System and the impact on student satisfaction." This will be conducted in an actual tertiary institution with well over 450 students; however, for our purposes, we will name the institution PDF Academy.

PDF Academy has its focus on on-line student administration via its Learning Management System (LMS) with a goal of attaining 1000 students enrolled both on campus and via distance learning. It is important to this establishment to have an LMS system, which can deliver the necessary information to students, lecturers, administrative and general staff. The LMS system has various modules and capabilities. These are listed below: -

- Enquiries and Application
- Registration and Training
- Curriculum Management
- Attendance and Tuition Management
- Assessment and Assignments
- Communication, class content and the knowledge repository

- Reporting (operational and management)
- Systems Administration.

The institute wishes to increase student enrolment via the LMS and to see an increase in the number of users among the current student population. Students currently enrolled in the institution have become disgruntled on several occasions due to failure to access current information on their grades for the previous semester to register for the upcoming semester, on-line, while off campus. They have also expressed a need for information on their payments, assignments, and assessments status.

Prospective students have expressed extreme difficulty in obtaining information on-line about programmes being offered by the institution, criterion for enrolment and the cost of the various courses. Considering these complaints, it was determined that a needs assessment would be in order as the institution has all the necessary programmes and staff in place to avert such problems.

The management of the institution believes that the necessary updates and data entry to the system is not being done. However, they would like to identify the area(s) at fault, rectify the situation, and at the same time get the students' views on how to better facilitate them and improve their organisation policies and service.

The proper handling of this student administration system is important to PDF Academy's new direction. All the preparation and implementation resources will be wasted if the issue is not resolved in a timely manner. The implications range from a decline in student population, lower levels of student satisfaction, the negative psychological effects on both the students and staff and the growth of the organisation as a learning organisation. PDF Academy invested millions of dollars in sourcing and developing this system and infrastructure. People were trained to make it successful. One may be tempted to assume that the system is the problem; however, there may be fundamental issues, which we aim to determine.

This assessment project seeks to determine whether the system processes, implemented by the organisation, are being followed, or if the inefficiencies with the system are directly related to the student administration staff and facilitators. It also seeks to identify whether students are satisfied with the Learning Management System and the institutions effort to monitor and update the system, and by extension transform the face of their learning experience.

Noted is the significance of this task and one seeks to resolve the issue in a timely and orderly fashion. Noteworthy is the fact that globally, organisations are moving towards online applications to guide and conduct training for their staff. Overall technology is the trend for all areas in the business and professional world. It is advantageous for PDF to understand and resolve this problem promptly.

Design Strategy

The Operational Audit and Organisational Climate assessment types were utilised to research the presenting problems at the Institution. These types were best able to facilitate the needed information as Operational Audit examines "organisation's structures, plans, objectives and how efficiently it uses its human and material resources... Operational Audits provides valuable information on the organisation's current operational condition" (Hurlock, 2015).

Organisational assessment focuses chiefly on work atmosphere and how it influences psychosomatic and emotional state. Incorporated within these types of assessments are varying data collection methods which include questionnaires, interviews, on-site observation, and focus groups.

The intended population was the 35 lecturing, administrative and technical staff of PDF Academy and the 450 on-campus students. The Assessment team administered questionnaires to 100 students, interviewed 10 staff members and further had a 'focus' group with another 10 of the remaining staff members.

On-site observation was incorporated to capture additional information and to broaden the scope of the assessment. Using simple random sampling, the nth interval was derived. The total population was divided by the total sampling size of 100 to give the interval (n) of 4.5. As such the assessment team administered the 100 questionnaires to every other fourth or fifth student encountered.

Care was taken to ensure sampling across the varied demographic characteristics, while not duplicating respondents. The same method was applied to the selection of staff members who were interviewed. This method was continued until all 10 interviews were conducted. Without any reference to established statistical procedures, ten staff members were asked to participate in the focus group. The team of Assessment

Specialists began on-site observation the moment they arrived at the institution.

Methodological triangulation was utilized to conduct this study, the process of mixing qualitative and quantitative 'methods' to sourcing data. This approach was chosen simply to make the study more comprehensive resulting from the complementary nature of the methods. Questionnaires were administered giving rise to the quantitative analysis while simultaneously interviews were conducted giving credence to the qualitative method.

Both methods are present with limitations such as the idea that qualitative research requires more time, greater clarity of goals and results cannot be analyzed by computer programs – hence subjected to researchers' opinions. Critics argue that quantitative research is too rigid, following a linear path, testing hypotheses linked to casual explanations (Nueman, 2003). It was hoped that utilizing both methods would combat the possible limitations of the other.

The team sought the cooperation of staff and students while management made available required resources. Data collection commenced with the distribution of questionnaires and the conducting of interviews with staff members. Focus groups were held and on-site observation occurred daily in the computer labs and student administration offices. After the initial two-month duration the team analysed the results and then presented the findings to management at the end of the third month. Recommendations were implemented at the start of the fourth month and changes began to occur within the fifth month.

Data Collection Methods

To ascertain the required information, the quantitative method of data collection was utilized with particular use of questionnaires as the primary method. The questionnaires were designed to gain as much information as possible thus they included closed-ended questions. The quantitative method was utilized as it seeks explanations and predictions that can be generalized to other persons and places. It establishes, confirms, or validate relationships and develop generalizations that contribute to our hypothesis.

Questionnaires were constructed in different sections to include the following: Section A, demographic data, Section B. which asked whether individuals had used the system and to what extent. Section C looked at whether individuals had experienced any problems and how these were handled or solved. This section asked respondents to indicate their satisfaction with the system and if they were indeed interested in utilising the system. They were constructed using variations of the Likert Scale; this rating scale is used to measure behaviour, attitude or other phenomenon of interest on a continuum ranging from "inadequate to excellent," never to always" or "strongly approve" to "strongly disapprove."

Interval scales were used to collect demographic data and Forced choice (yes/no) questions were used when one answer had more than one response. Questionnaires were administered on an individual basis; therefore, participants were given enough time to complete and return the questionnaire immediately thus eliminating any loss of data.

A total of five persons canvassed the institution and surveyed every 5th student encountered. This was very successful as all persons readily participated resulting in all required 100 questionnaires been answered or received.

The secondary source of data collection method utilized was the qualitative method with special emphasis on the use of interviews. Interviews were used to gain more sensitive information and garner opinions on issues requiring explanations.

Two separate interview schedules were utilised. The first was used to gauge the responses of students visiting the computer labs to use the systems. This medium asked key question that directly influenced the findings as to what caused difficulties in the first instance. Queries ranged from asking whether respondents were students with a system password to whether they had knowledge of the system and if they ever attempted to access the system. The respondents were randomly selected without statistical inference resulting in a larger majority canvassed. Most persons approached responded except for five who were either too upset to be rational or were simply not interested.

The other interview schedule captured information from staff members. It sought their opinions on the system, its functions and whether they had received reports from the students or other user as well as how they may have responded to the reports. These interviews were conducted by the Project Coordinator who interviewed every 3rd staff member or lecturer based on the 'nth' rule of systematic random sampling.

Of note is the fact that these persons offered suggestions which will be highlighted in the section recommendations, although some suggestions were clearly opinionated

Additional information was sought using the method of observation using an observation schedule designed to capture data on the use of the system by students or other users. Pertinent points such as number of users of the system, how successful they were in registering for courses when such attempt was made, length of time spent on the system and whether they could manipulate the system were ticked off over a 5 – 8-hour shift.

These approaches were chosen simply to make the study more comprehensive resulting from the complementary nature of the methods. Questions garnered from the questionnaires gave rise to the quantitative analysis while simultaneously interviews were conducted giving credence to the qualitative method.

Findings   Figure 4.1

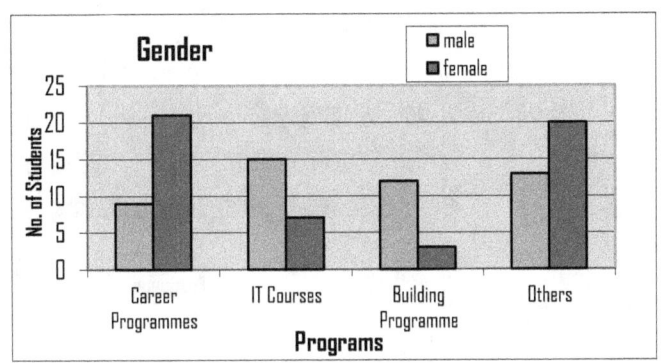

The graph shows the ratio of males to females in the sample. It is fair to conclude that there were as many males as there were females. There was a total of 51 females to 49 males. However, both males and females each had a higher total in two categories. Males dominated the traditional courses such as Building and IT programmes. The Career programmes had a greater total of females and the comprehensive tally of the other programs also had more females.   Figure 4.2

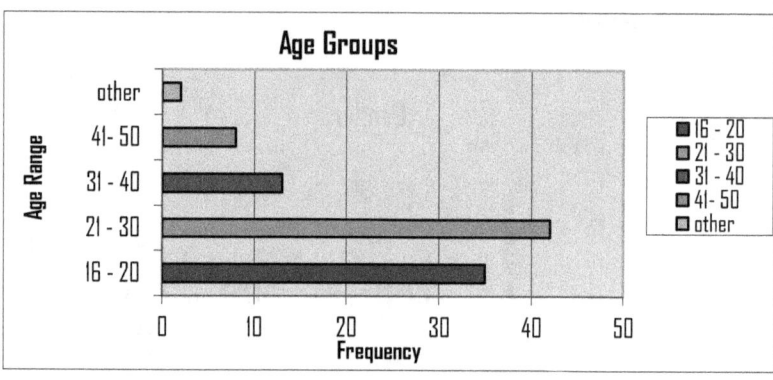

On this chart one readily sees the age ranges of the participants in the study. The range of 21 - 30 had the largest number of respondents of 42%, followed by the range 16 – 20 with 35%, while the range 31 – 40 had 13%. The age range 41 – 50 showed 8% of the sample. The category 'other' had the least number of participants with 2% of the total.

Figure 4.3

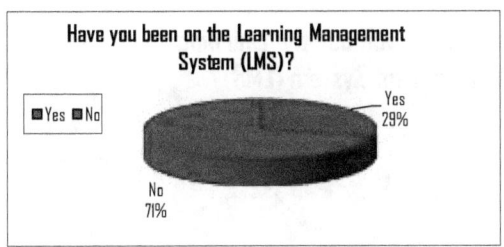

The pie chart above is proportioned to represent the percentage of respondents that had been on the Learning Management System. It indicates that the larger part of the sample 71% indicated they had not utilised the system. A meagre 29% of the participants indicated having used the system.

Figure 4.4

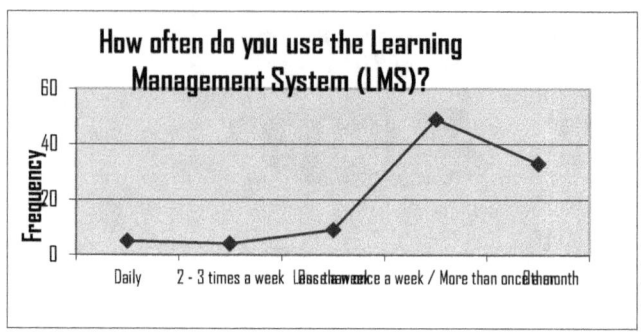

Of the total 29% of persons who used the system 49% used the system less than once a week or more than once a month. 33% were in the category other and these persons indicated using the system at the beginning and end of each semester. 9% of the respondents used it once a week while 5% used the system daily; another 4% used the system 2 – 3 times a week.

Figure 4.5

Was the problem solved or addressed

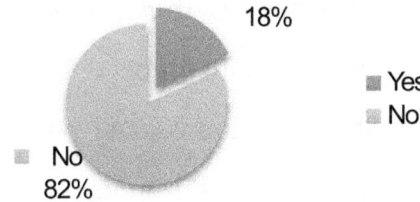

Yes
18%

■ Yes
▓ No

▓ No
82%

Responses to one of the more pertinent questions asked, indicated that problems reported by a significant 82% of the students were not resolved. A low percentage of 18% of the sample stated that their problems were dealt with or resolved.

There were three questions which enquired on the level of satisfaction of the students. A large percentage of the population, 76% agreed that "I am very interested in using the Learning Management System (LMS) to access my grades and attendance records online." Of the three choices five percent of the sample agreed "I am satisfied with the manner in which the Learning Management System (LMS) is handled." Less than three percent (3%) were satisfied with the statement of "I am satisfied with the assistance given to me so that I can use the Learning Management System (LMS)."

The findings collected from the interviews indicated that an average 85% of the staff members believe they are being unfairly asked to perform too many tasks on the LMS. Of the 35 instructors interviewed 10% had never been on the system and another 55% had not been on the system in over a month. 20% of the staff indicated that they are up to date in entering information on the system.

When asked whether students had reported to them issues, they were having with the system, 85% stated that students did but with a measly 35% doing anything to resolve the issues themselves. Another 20% reported it to the Student Administrative office or to the Systems Administrator. These lecturers indicated one major issue being asked to post test and examination results on the system which was an added strain resulting from their current workload.

Instructors recommended that other staff personnel be used to assist with the task of entering grades, as this would speed up the process. They also indicated that they be exempted from assessing exams so that they may prepare and enter the following semesters timetable and course work. Part time instructors suggested that paid time be allotted in their contractual agreement for them to do all the extra tasks required of them, as it relates to the system.

Upon observing the student administrative persons at the front office, it was noted that the reception area was being manned by two staff members, who at various intervals during the day were occupied with playing computer games. During the observation period it was noted that only two (2) of the senior persons were able to handle the student issues with the system, and they were not interfacing the students at any time. 95% of the time students were told to fill out a form which sat on the counter and was never passed on to the relevant persons.

The students who were interviewed expressed that it was very difficult for them to see their issues resolved. 85% had problems with their login information and password. 10% attempted to log on to the system with their email password from other systems and 5% did not attempt to collect the information from the student admin office. It was noted from the student observation session in the computer labs and library that 45% of the students who used the facility attempted to get on to the LMS. Of that 45%, only 20% were successful in login on and were often not able to register to their courses as these were not posted to the system. Most persons took over 30 minutes to access or utilise the system for simple procedures such as checking grades, assignments or registering.

Majority of the students needing to use the program became frustrated at not being able to log on to the system and often 'venting' sessions ensued. They vehemently expressed their 'fed-up-ness' of the system and often stated that the system be 'dash weh'. Some expressed that the procedure for making complaints about the system needs simplification.

Analysis and Discussion

Outlined below is an analysis and discussion of the data that was gathered using the methodology previously outlined in conformity to what obtains in good research practices. In the previous chapter, the findings were represented on graphs and charts, which were colour coded with legends provided for ease of interpretation. Each section of the questionnaire was aptly represented and separately analysed with our inference along with the comparisons made to existing literature.

After exhaustive correlation of information various operational anomalies were apparent. In any system of this nature information is essential to the smooth delivery of services. If for any reason the information is not reaching the system in a timely manner, then there is bound to be a level of dissatisfaction among users of the system. Further to this, persons using the system became frustrated when they are unable to complete tasks that the system was set up to do. Added to this is the fact that this service is being offered at a cost to the students.

Our sampled population of 100 students was broken down into 49 males and 51 females. Most of these persons fell between the ages of 16 and 30, they accounted for 77% of the total. 13% percent comprised the age range 31 – 40 while the remaining 10% included the 41 and over category. We believe that this is an adequate sample as all the respondents were students of the PDF Academy.

Most of these persons were educated beyond the Secondary level with 13% attaining graduate or postgraduate education. They indicated that 75% were full time students and the other 25% were part time. This tie into Evans (2000) in his article "<u>Workers in the new economy: Organisation for Economic Cooperation and Development</u>", He expresses the sentiments that it is important to remember that to ensure prosperity, people have the necessities including education. It is an important priority of the Institution to invest in further education and training to raise the level and quality of their students. We also sought to find out whether the sampled population were regular users of the LMS to which an overwhelming 71% indicated they did not. A significant 29% however were involved.

Jarvis (2003) has suggested that, "human beings have a basic need to learn, and that they are lifelong learners and the provision of education across the lifespan is one way by which people can satisfy this basic need". Hence, the various levels of training provided and the usage of the online application the Learning Management System to track users throughout their learning career. However, this system would not be successful if it is not managed properly, and the users shown the value and purpose of the system. With the institution's emphasis on online applications to facilitate access and steer the management aspect of their business, it became paramount to pose the question. Therefore, the representative figure indicating that 76% agreed "I am very interested in using the Learning Management System (LMS) to access my grades and attendance records online" is especially important as it shows some indication that the students would give the system and the institution another chance.

Section C was one of the critical areas of the questionnaire as it asked for the respondent's agreement to several key areas to the research topic. It looked at whether persons had experienced any problems and how these were resolved if at all. This section asked respondents to signify their satisfaction with the LMS and to indicate whether they were interested in utilizing the system. Questions were constructed using variations of the Likert Scale; the rating scale used to measure opinions and interest. Online applications are important to the future success of any organisation that seeks to cut cost, increase productivity while empowering their students to excel in their work.

The responses to varying questions affected the margin of generalisation given in the implications and recommendations sections. As the sampled participants for the research numbered 100, each participant is equivalent to 4.5% of the total research population. Each response therefore counts and plays an essential role to the outcome.

Overall, as was mentioned, we are satisfied with the data we were able to generate in the time available. Most of the questions were easily interpreted. Performing a pre-test was very helpful before the final study; with the time available at our disposal, it was indeed possible to conduct a pre-test. The decision to not do a pre-test would have provided too many disadvantages. Namely, improvements or suggested changes would not have been made to the questionnaire until during the process. We ensured that these suggestions were captured by the facilitator. In most cases, questions required little clarification. We ensured to request that participants read the questions and the corresponding options slowly and carefully.

This chapter seeks to present implications and recommendations realised from the needs assessment. Information has been presented on the research design and chosen methodology. Further, we have displayed or represented findings, results and observations collated from both the quantitative and qualitative methods used. Then lastly, as in the previous chapter we sought to adeptly analyse and discuss the results.

In analysing the data collected from this assessment we have reached the conclusion that the quality of responses to the questionnaire is satisfactory. These responses will affect the implications and recommendations we sought to give from this study. Seeking to provide implications derived from the three sections of the questionnaire and promptly addressing several of the key areas, recommendations will be given on the future of the PDF Academy and how best to implement and measure the effectiveness of the recommendations.

While analysing the generated data, it appeared to the researchers that information derived from the interview was not separate from that captured by the questionnaires, as they both complimented each other. The interview was conducted face-to-face which allowed us to capture, non-verbal cues, such as facial expressions and body gestures, which would otherwise have been missed. This allowed the interviewers to know which direction to move in.

There are recommendations, which have been generated from the questionnaire responses, as well as from the interviews and observations. We have attempted to outline these with a summary explanation following.

Recommendations being pro-offered:

- Communicate clearly, the benefits and opportunities to be derived from the online application, (Learning Management System) to both staff and students of the institution.

- From the statistics more persons were dissatisfied than those very satisfied with the institutions handling of issues and overall approach. Create room for improvement in these areas.

- Initiatives, steps, goals, and objectives of PDF's should be clearly communicated to the persons involved.

- Create avenues for staff to practice what is learnt on the system and for frequent follow up and retraining to be done, for satisfactoriness to improve.

The opportunities, to be derived from on the online application, should be clearly and precisely communicated to both staff and students of the institution. This will facilitate the acceptance of the system and ensure some level of cooperation from both staff and students. It is integral that these persons understand the goals and objectives of the company so that they may play their part in the advancement of the institution and not be a detractor of it.

From the statistics more persons were dissatisfied than those very satisfied with the institution's approach and handling of the system so far. There is always room for improvement in this area. A satisfied student or staff member is a productive worker and as highlighted in the first recommendations goals should be made clear, but not only so, these goals when accomplished should have equally clear and attainable rewards. The procedures implemented to clarify or attain these goals should not be arduous or labouring to the individuals.

Initiatives, steps, goals, and objectives of PDF's should be clearly communicated to the persons involved. Not just the initiatives towards using the online application but also in accordance with every aspect and dealings of the Academy. If this measure has already been taken, then it needs to be adhered to and possibly made more visible at the institution.

Create avenues for staff to practice what is learnt on the system and for frequent follow up and retraining to be done, for satisfactoriness to improve. If workers are generally of the opinion that on the (LMS) brings in additional work volume, then it may be the reflexive action to shun it. However, if there were opportunities and sufficient time presented for the worker to enter data or play their respective roles as it relates to the system, this would promote job satisfaction and satisfactoriness.

Utilize the reception staff in posting of test and examination results. After the beginning of lectures each morning reception will be manned by one staff while the other collects work to be posted from the lecturers out trays. This will unburden the instructors from performing the many tasks they have to, daily; however, still let the verification duties lie with them.

Retraining should be held in the use of the system, paying strict attention to the level of computer literacy, and age of participants also ensuring that the groups are as homogenous as possible and of a manageable size. This will ensure all users are at a comfortable level with the system. They should be trained in areas which will allow any one of them to resolve an issue from a student if it arises.

Access to the system should be given via the student's id number and his/her selected password. Many students do not initially have an email address and some even forget the assigned one. Therefore, the student already accesses the computer facility using his or her ID and they also have identification cards with the number. Therefore, it is unlikely they will forget this important number. In this regard the access codes would be friendlier to all students. There should be ample and timely notification of any further changes to the codes.

There should be a one telephone contact number, one E-mail address and one written message drop off point, established for complaints. Complaints should be processed and addressed promptly and openly. These may also be directed to the respective persons. Forms may include the issue facing the students and automatically filter it to the respective individual for timely and prompt processing.

These recommendations if followed will assist in providing and implementing a concrete solution for the Academy's issues and see the institution attaining and surpassing their objectives. It is integral that a senior person of the institution directly oversees this application and any issue relating to it.

For any learning organisation that implements a software system which helps to streamline and improve some of their student administrative processes, it is important to occasionally conduct a needs analysis of the various procedures. Therefore, this exercise of evaluating the Learning Management System efficiency and staff proficiency in using the system, on student satisfaction levels is geared towards providing pivotal insight into the executive decisions and the outcomes of implementing such strategies.

PDF Academy operates as one of Jamaica's tertiary training facility with 450 students. The institution has as its focus an on-line student administration, Learning Management System (LMS) with a goal of attaining 1000 student enrolment both on campus and via distance learning. It is important to this institution to have an LMS system, which can deliver and obtaining the necessary information to students, lecturers, administrative and general staff.

The Operational Audit and Organisational Climate assessment types were selected to research the presenting problems at the Institution. These types were best able to facilitate the needed information. Organisational assessment focuses chiefly on work atmosphere and how it influences psychosomatic and emotional state. Incorporated within these types of assessments are varying data collection methods which include questionnaires, interviews, on-site observation, and focus groups.

The quantitative method of data collection was utilized with particular use of questionnaires as the primary method, to determine the required information. Questionnaires were designed to gain as much information as possible thus they included closed-ended questions. It validates relationships and develops generalizations that contribute to our hypothesis.

Recommendations were generated from the questionnaire, interviews, and observations. These included that clear communication of opportunities to be derived from on the online application were to be expressed. Persons were largely dissatisfied with the institutions handling of issues and overall approach. Improvements were to be made in these areas. Goals and objectives of the Academy's should be clearly communicated to the persons involved. Avenues were to be created for staff to practice what is learnt on the system and for

frequent follow up and retraining to be done,
for satisfactoriness to improve.

Reference

Evans, J. (2000). Workers in the new
economy: Organisation for Economic
Cooperation and Development. The
OECD Observer, Retrieved from
http://www.findarticles.cornlp/articl
es/mi ga3648

Hurlock, C., (2005). Lecture Notes: Planning
and Designing Needs Assessment.
VTDI: Kingston

Jarvis, P. (2003). Adult & Continuing
Education: Theory and Practice (2nd
Ed.). RoutledgeFalmer.

Kaufman, R., Rojas, A., M., and Mayer, H.,
(1993). Needs Assessment: A User's
Guide. New Jersey: Pfeiffer.

McNamara, C., (1999). Basic Guide to
Program Evaluation. Retrieved from
http://www.managementhelp.org/ev
aluatn/fnl_eval.htm

Neuman, W. (2003). Social Research Methods;
    Qualitative and Quantitative
    Approaches (5th Ed.). Boston, Allyn
    and Bacon.

Remember, "the heights by great men reached and kept were not attained by sudden flight, but they, while their companions slept, were toiling upward in the night." – Henry Wadsworth Longfellow.

Denise N. Fyffe

… is an author, educator, and Christian minister whose understanding of workplace culture was shaped not in theory, but through years of lived experience inside Jamaican institutions, tertiary environments, and corporate learning spaces. Her professional journey has taken her through organizations with strong systems and those with fragile ones, giving her a front-row seat to the realities of workplace theft, leadership gaps, human behavior, and the quiet emotional toll these issues leave behind.

Born and raised in Kingston, Jamaica, Denise carries the resilience, cultural insight, and grounded wisdom of the communities that shaped her—Harbour View, Windward Road, Rockfort, and Seaview Gardens. These early experiences taught her how people navigate pressure, how trust is built and broken, and how integrity becomes a daily practice rather than an abstract ideal.

With more than two decades of experience across education, training, publishing, and ministry, Denise has worked in environments where systems were strong and transparent, and in others where vulnerabilities created opportunities for misconduct. These contrasting realities deepened her understanding of organizational behavior and inspired her commitment to helping institutions build cultures of trust, accountability, and protection.

She is the founder of RTCLM Ministry, RTCLM Academy and Foundation as well as Jamaica Pen Publishers; where she mentors writers, develops leaders, and creates resources that strengthen both individuals and organizations. Her work blends cultural awareness, spiritual grounding, and practical guidance, offering readers clarity in environments that often feel overwhelming or uncertain.

Across more than 90 published books, Denise has explored themes of emotional wellness, spiritual growth, family life, and personal resilience. In this book, she brings together her professional experience, her ministry perspective, and her lived encounters with workplace systems to offer a rare, honest, and deeply human look at integrity in the modern workplace.

Denise continues to write, teach, and minister with a heart for service and a commitment to helping people and organizations thrive with dignity, wisdom, and purpose.

RECOMMENDED BOOKS

All books are available at online book retailers.

Dear Reader

Thank you for reading this book.

It means so much that you have taken the time out of your busy schedule. Nothing makes us happier than knowing that someone is reading, and hopefully enjoying, what took us many months, even years, to create.

Please stay with us on this journey. We welcome your feedback, opinions, and suggestions about the book. We would appreciate a few lines of review on the website where you purchased this book.

You can also write us a note at Jamaica Pen Publishing on Facebook, or Twitter or contact us via our website.